CHAKRAS

A COLORFUL GUIDE FOR CHILDREN

THE SACRED BOOKSHELF

FOR AMORA AND ALEXAVIER

WITH ALL OF OUR LOVE.

-MOMMY & DADDY

WHAT ARE CHAKRAS?

CHAKRAS ARE COLORFUL ENERGY WHEELS IN OUR BODIES.

WE ALL HAVE MANY CHAKRAS,

HOWEVER WE HAVE 7 MAIN CHAKRAS.

THEY START FROM THE BASE OF OUR SPINES

AND GO UP TO THE TOPS OF OUR HEADS.

THEY'RE THE POWER CENTERS THAT HELP
US FEEL HAPPY AND HEALTHY WHEN THEY
ARE IN BALANCE AND UNBLOCKED.

IMAGINE YOUR BODY IS LIKE A MAGICAL GARDEN,
AND HIDDEN INSIDE ARE YOUR CHAKRAS.
JUST LIKE TREES NEED SUNLIGHT AND WATER TO GROW,
OUR CHAKRAS NEED LOVE AND GOOD FEELINGS
TO SHINE BRIGHT.

WHEN OUR CHAKRAS ARE OUT OF BALANCE
IT CAN CAUSE US TO NOT FEEL OR
EXPRESS OURSELVES IN THE BEST WAY.

LET'S EXPLORE EACH ONE OF OUR 7 CHAKRAS,
SEE WHAT CAN HAPPEN WHEN THEY'RE OUT OF BALANCE,
AND LEARN SPECIAL AFFIRMATIONS
TO HELP RECHARGE AND REALIGN THEM.

THE MULADHARA CHAKRA

THIS IS OUR FIRST CHAKRA.

IT'S ALSO CALLED
THE ROOT CHAKRA

IT IS RED AND IT'S LOCATED AT
THE BASE OF OUR SPINE.

THE ROOT CHAKRA HELPS YOU FEEL GROUNDED, LIKE THE
ROOTS OF A TREE.
WHEN IT IS BALANCED YOU FEEL SAFE,
SECURE AND STRONG.

IT ALSO HELPS US TO FEEL
CONNECTED TO OUR FAMILY, FRIENDS, AND ANCESTORS.

WHEN IT'S OUT OF BALANCE: YOU MIGHT FEEL SCARED OR WORRIED.

TO BALANCE YOUR ROOT CHAKRA, IMAGINE A BRIGHT RED LIGHT AT THE BASE OF YOUR SPINE AND REPEAT THIS AFFIRMATION

"I AM SAFE AND SECURE."

THE SVADHISTHANA CHAKRA

THIS IS OUR SECOND CHAKRA.

IT'S ALSO CALLED
THE SACRAL CHAKRA

IT IS ORANGE AND IT'S LOCATED
BELOW OUR BELLY BUTTONS.

THE SACRAL CHAKRA IS
BRIGHT LIKE THE RISING SUN.
ITS ALL ABOUT CREATIVITY AND JOY.

IT HELPS YOU ENJOY FUN ACTIVITIES LIKE
DRAWING AND DANCING.

WHEN IT IS BALANCED YOU FEEL
CREATIVE, HAPPY, AND ABLE
TO EXPRESS FEELINGS FREELY.

WHEN IT'S OUT OF BALANCE: YOU MIGHT FEEL SAD OR HAVE TROUBLE HAVING FUN.

TO BALANCE YOUR SACRAL CHAKRA, IMAGINE A BRIGHT ORANGE LIGHT GLOWING BELOW YOUR BELLY BUTTON AND REPEAT THIS AFFIRMATION

"I AM CREATIVE AND JOYFUL."

THE MANIPURA CHAKRA

THIS IS OUR THIRD CHAKRA.

IT'S ALSO CALLED
THE SOLAR PLEXUS CHAKRA

IT IS YELLOW AND IT'S LOCATED
IN OUR TUMMIES.

THE **SOLAR PLEXUS** CHAKRA IS
BRIGHT LIKE A SUNFLOWER IN BLOOM.

HAVE YOU EVER FELT BUTTERFLIES IN YOUR TUMMY WHEN
YOU'RE EXCITED?
THAT'S YOUR **SOLAR PLEXUS**!

WHEN IT IS BALANCED IT BOOSTS OUR CONFIDENCE, COURAGE,
AND SELF-WORTH.

WHEN IT'S OUT OF BALANCE: YOU MIGHT FEEL SHY OR AFRAID TO TRY NEW THINGS.

TO BALANCE YOUR **SOLAR PLEXUS** CHAKRA, IMAGINE A BRIGHT **YELLOW** LIGHT GLOWING IN YOUR TUMMY, AND REPEAT THIS AFFIRMATION

"I AM CONFIDENT AND BRAVE."

THE ANAHATA CHAKRA

THIS IS OUR FOURTH CHAKRA.

IT'S ALSO CALLED
THE HEART CHAKRA

IT IS GREEN AND IT'S LOCATED
AT THE CENTER OF OUR CHEST.

THE **HEART** CHAKRA IS
LIKE A LUSH **GREEN** GARDEN

ITS ABOUT LOVE, KINDNESS, AND COMPASSION.

WHEN IT IS BALANCED IT HELPS US TO FEEL AND SHARE LOVE WITH OTHERS LIKE OUR FAMILIES, FRIENDS, PETS, AND EVEN OURSELVES.

WHEN IT'S OUT OF BALANCE: YOU MIGHT FEEL LONELY OR HAVE TROUBLE BEING KIND AND GETTING ALONG WITH OTHERS.

"I AM LOVING AND KIND."

THE VISHUDDHA CHAKRA

THIS IS OUR FIFTH CHAKRA.

IT'S ALSO CALLED
THE THROAT CHAKRA

IT IS BLUE AND IT'S LOCATED IN OUR THROATS.

THE **THROAT** CHAKRA IS
LIKE A CLEAR **BLUE** SKY.

ITS ABOUT EXPRESSING YOURSELF AND COMMUNICATION.
ITS LIKE A MICROPHONE FOR YOUR FEELINGS
AND THOUGHTS, HELPING YOU TO SHARE
THEM WITH THOSE AROUND US.

WHEN IT IS BALANCED WE COMMUNICATE CLEARLY,
SPEAK HONESTLY, AND EVEN SING LOUD AND PROUD.

WHEN IT'S OUT OF BALANCE: YOU MIGHT HAVE TROUBLE SPEAKING UP OR SAYING WHAT YOU FEEL.

TO BALANCE YOUR THROAT CHAKRA, IMAGINE A BLUE LIGHT GLOWING IN YOUR NECK, AND REPEAT THIS AFFIRMATION

"I SPEAK MY TRUTH."

THE AJNA CHAKRA

THIS IS OUR SIXTH CHAKRA.

IT'S ALSO CALLED
THE THIRD EYE CHAKRA

IT IS INDIGO AND IT'S LOCATED
ON OUR FOREHEADS, BETWEEN OUR EYES.

THE THIRD EYE CHAKRA IS LIKE OUR
INNER SUPER HERO

CLOSE YOUR EYES AND PICTURE A DEEP DARK BLUE
NIGHT SKY FILLED WITH TWINKLING STARS.
THAT'S OUR THIRD EYE CHAKRA!

IT HELPS US UNDERSTAND AND CONNECT WITH
THE WORLD AROUND US.

WHEN IT IS BALANCED WE TRUST OUR INTUITION
AND HAVE A VIVID IMAGINATION.

WHEN IT'S OUT OF BALANCE: YOU MIGHT FEEL CONFUSED OR HAVE TROUBLE MAKING DECISIONS.

TO OPEN YOUR **THIRD EYE** CHAKRA, IMAGINE
AN **INDIGO** LIGHT GLOWING ON YOUR FOREHEAD, AND
REPEAT THIS AFFIRMATION

"I TRUST MY INTUITION."

THE SAHASRARA CHAKRA

THIS IS OUR SEVENTH CHAKRA.
ITS ALSO CALLED
THE CROWN CHAKRA

IT IS VIOLET OR SOMETIMES WHITE AND IT'S
LOCATED AT THE TOP OF OUR HEADS.

THE **CROWN** CHAKRA IS
IS LIKE A SPARKLING MAGICAL CROWN MADE
WITH SHINY GEMS SITTING ON TOP OF OUR HEADS.

WHEN ITS BALANCED,
IT CONNECTS US TO THE UNIVERSE AND
ALL OF ITS WONDERS. WE FEEL CONNECTED
TO EVERYTHING AND EVERYONE AROUND US.

WHEN IT IS OPEN, WE CONNECT TO
SOMETHING BIGGER THAN OURSELVES.

WHEN IT'S OUT OF BALANCE: YOU MIGHT FEEL DISCONNECTED OR ALONE.

TO ENERGIZE YOUR CROWN CHAKRA,
IMAGINE A BRIGHT VIOLET OR WHITE LIGHT SHINING
ABOVE YOUR HEAD,
AND REPEAT THIS AFFIRMATION

"I AM CONNECTED TO EVERYTHING."

JUST LIKE TAKING CARE OF A
GARDEN HELPS PLANTS GROW,
WE CAN TAKE CARE OF OUR CHAKRAS
BY BEING KIND TO OURSELVES AND OTHERS,
EATING HEALTHY FOODS, PLAYING,
LAUGHING, AND SPENDING TIME WITH LOVED ONES.

WHEN OUR CHAKRAS ARE HAPPY,
WE FEEL HAPPY TOO.

REMEMBER YOUR CHAKRAS ARE ALWAYS WITH YOU.
TAKING CARE OF THEM WITH
AFFIRMATIONS AND MEDITATION HELPS
YOU STAY HAPPY, STRONG, AND FULL OF MAGIC.

EVERY DAY CAN BE A NEW ADVENTURE WITH YOUR
POWERFUL CHAKRAS!